ENVIRONMENTAL SYST

Arid Lands

D. C. Money

Evans

Evans Brothers Limited

Published by Evans Brothers Limited
Montague House, Russell Square, London WC1B 5BX

Evans Brothers (Nigeria Publishers) Limited
PMB 5164, Jericho Road, Ibadan

First published 1982

Acknowledgements
Eric Kay pp. 21 (below), 31, 38, 41
FAO p. 28
Popperfoto pp. 15, 26, 40 and front cover
John Topham Picture Library pp. 21 (above), 25, 43
V. C. Robertson p. 35 (above)

All other photos were taken by the author

Line illustrations by Reproduction Drawings

Filmset and printed in Great Britain by
BAS Printers Limited, Over Wallop, Hampshire

ISBN 0 237 29269 6 PRA 7295

Contents

Cover photograph This Saharan landscape admirably illustrates the processes of physical disintegration, the presence of water in some form, and the survival of specially adapted forms of vegetation, which characterise the arid lands. The conditions which favour such massive splitting are described on p. 22, and the ability of plants to obtain atmospheric moisture and water from rock storage on p. 12.

A Systems Approach

The definition and examination of systems, more or less simplified for study purposes, enables the complexities of the real, observed world to be considered in an orderly manner. We can see more clearly the interrelationships between the components of a system and the flows of energy and matter which take place within it. We simplify to see how the system is structured and to consider how the components may further be studied and measured. Simplifications involve subjective actions, and it is up to us to define the limits of study and specify the systems and sub-systems under consideration.

We can elect to study a large arid ecosystem such as the Namib Desert, or a more restricted ecosystem such as an oasis, and within these can examine separate interacting soil and plant systems; or we may investigate smaller sub-systems involving, say, the relationships between root activity and nutrient release from surrounding soil material. In each case we may identify independent key variables, external to the system yet affecting the flows of matter and energy within—such as the atmospheric temperature and humidity which affect the weathering of the rocks, or man's input of energy as he puts irrigation water into the system and forms nutrient solutions. Everything is related to everything else to a greater or lesser degree, and we try to establish the most important relationships within whatever system we define, and to identify the variables which control these relationships.

Matter and energy pass continuously through a mature ecosystem, and within it the plant and animal organisms and the elements of their habitat are approximately in a state of equilibrium. In arid environments, however, any mature state may be easily disturbed. The natural equilibrium is upset by the animals which support a nomadic group, as well as by the inputs and activities needed to maintain a permanent settlement. Most chains of activity instigated by man are extremely complex. A systems approach enables us initially to isolate human components and consider in turn other variables of the atmosphere, hydrosphere, lithosphere and biosphere.

A surprisingly large number of plants—some with long life cycles, some ephemeral, some actively growing, some dormant—occur in arid and semi-arid regions, for desert rocks are not necessarily low in plant nutrients, though the conditions which make them available to plants may only occasionally be present. The supply of nutrients involves exchanges between soil systems and vegetation systems. So we look first at an arid system within which are interacting plant and soil sub-systems. We may then focus both on these internal interactions and on the main groups of external variables which affect them. The vegetation itself has important influences on other surface features.

The Vegetation-Soil System

Figs. 1 and 2 show an open system and the direction of exchanges of energy and matter with its environment. The chosen internal component systems are those of plants and the soil. Climatic elements are among the external independent variables affecting them: by controlling, for example, the rates of weathering of rocks and the release of plant nutrients from mineral particles. For instance, characteristically large diurnal temperature ranges stimulate mechanical weathering; and after prolonged drought, the brief periods of torrential rainfall cause strong mechanical and chemical weathering. Even when there is no rainfall, the atmospheric moisture may be sufficient to cause dew to form at night and so encourage chemical weathering.

We must consider the nature of the exchanges between rocks, soils and plants, and the flow of nutrients which support vegetation and so affect landform development and human activities in the arid lands. Although the atmospheric elements carbon, hydrogen, oxygen and nitrogen make up 95 per cent of the dry weight of protoplasm in plants, over forty other elements are needed by most living organisms. Chemical weathering of the rocks and mineral particles make such elements available to plants. Calcium, magnesium, potassium, nitrogen, phosphorus, sulphur, silicon, iron and aluminium are widely available from rock sources, though a given soil may lack a particular element. Weathering releases other elements which plants may require in very small amounts, but which are vital to their development—such as

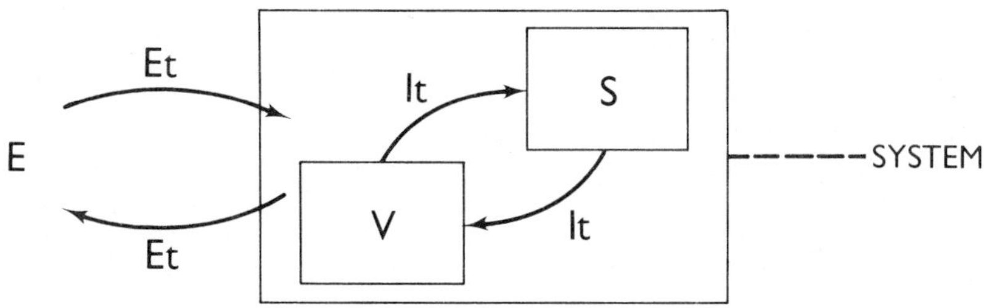

Transfers of energy/mass t

Control variables: External E; Internal I

Sub-system
V Vegetation
S Soil

Fig. 1 A selected system with internal transfers, such as nutrient exchanges, between the soil and vegetation sub-systems, and external transfers, such as solar energy inputs and transpiration losses to the atmosphere.

manganese, zinc, copper and cobalt. In solution, these metal cations may pass into plants in exchange for hydrogen ions released from rootlets.

The nutrients released from solution are temporarily 'stored' in plants, together with the elements received from photosynthetic and nitrifying processes. They are returned to the surface in plant litter. When this decomposes, it releases them to the soil. It also provides organic acids,

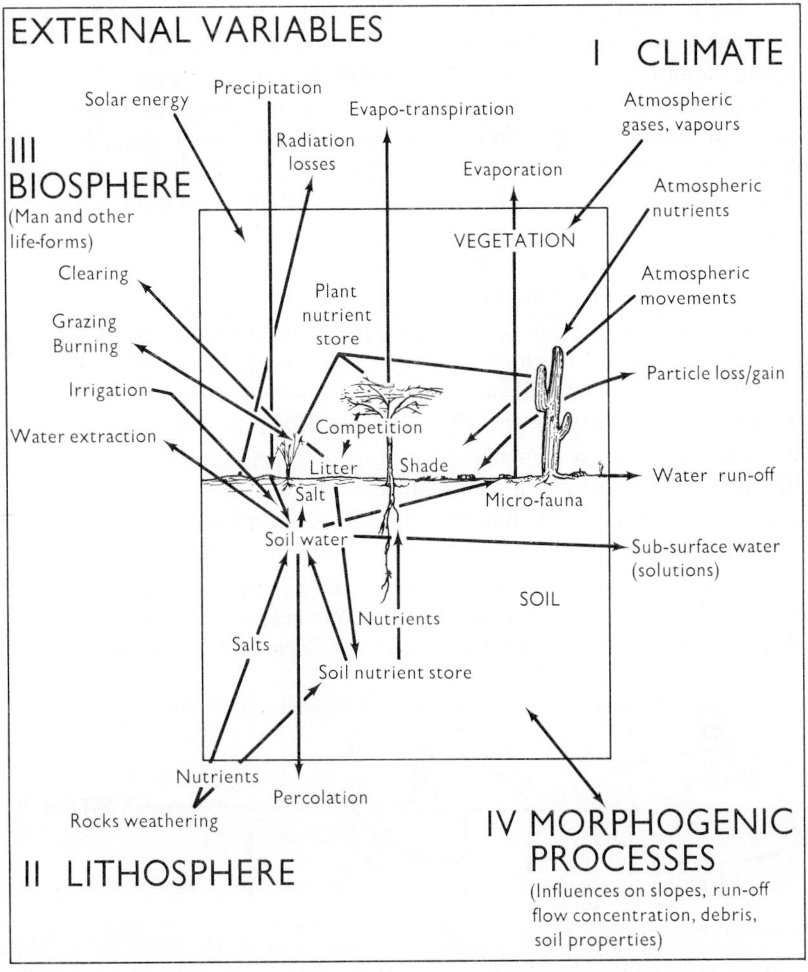

Fig. 2 To appreciate how variables affect a soil–vegetation system, we choose four broad categories (I–IV). For example, we can look in more detail at changes within the system due to: I climatic fluctuations; II minerals released by weathering; III over-use of vegetation or water resources; IV dune encroachment. The variables interact, but their particular influences can be seen in isolation.

which may act on minerals and so help weather the bedrock.

In very dry locations it is difficult for soils to develop, for both wind and sheet run-off after torrential rain transport particles from dry surfaces. However, in the semi-arid lands with well-defined rainy seasons a soil may develop recognisable horizons and have a moderate organic content. Brief periods of leaching occur after rainstorms, though persistent drought causes upwards movement of soil solutions and evaporation leaves salts within the soils, or forms saline crusts (p. 19).

Plants must adapt to such processes. So we look in turn, from page 16 onwards, at how climatic and other variables affect the working of the internal plant–soil system. Those which form part of the surrounding environment include local rock types (lithological features) and many biotic variables, including man and wild and domestic animals. All of these may transfer matter and energy across the boundary of the system (Fig. 2).

Definition of Arid Lands

It is not easy to define arid lands precisely. Sometimes rainfall amounts are used to indicate desert conditions, such as 'those areas where mean precipitation is less than 250 mm a year'. But where the rainfall is so erratic, averages mean little; also arid conditions occur in both temperate and tropical regions, where there are very different rates of evaporation.

The word 'desert' is often used to describe a region of extreme aridity. It is also used to imply a deserted place, with few inhabitants, in such terms as 'white desert' (ice-covered area) or 'green desert' (dense rainforest). Many of the dry lands described as deserts are certainly not devoid of vegetation—the Gibson Desert and other very dry parts of Australia, for example—though lack of continuous vegetation is an indicator of aridity. The word 'arid', meaning parched or dry, is vague in itself; and so, therefore, are descriptions such a 'semi-arid'. Moreover, it is seldom possible to point out on the ground the exact limits of a desert, nor recognise the boundaries of areas classified as deserts by climatologists.

There are advantages, however, in using empirical climatic systems of classification, such as those of Thornthwaite and Köppen.[1] Thornthwaite determined the boundary separating arid from semi-arid areas by comparing the potential evapo-transpiration (PEt), that is the amount of water lost from plants, assuming that water were always available to the roots, with the precipitation (P). Thus, when P = PEt the index is 0; when there is no precipitation the index is −100; and when P is far greater then PEt it is +100. Generally, climates with values −20 to −40 are considered semi-arid, and those below −40 are arid.

Köppen used simpler formulae, like those below, where r = mean annual rainfall (cm) and t = mean annual temperature (°C). In his climatic code, **B** zones are dry ones, where, on average, evaporation exceeds precipitation throughout the year. **BW** climates are those of the desert (waste) and **BS** those of semi-arid areas. The **BW/BS** boundary passes through points where the value 1 is obtained from the formulae shown below; the **BS**/Humid region boundary passes through those where the value 2 is obtained.

	formula	BW/BS	BS/Humid
winter precipitation maximum	r/t	$=1$	$=2$
evenly distributed precipitation	$r/(t+7)$	$=1$	$=2$
summer precipitation maximum	$r/(t+14)$	$=1$	$=2$

The graphs in Fig. 3 illustrate these relationships and emphasise that in hot lands with summer rainfall and high evaporation rates there may be desert conditions even when the mean annual rainfall is over 400 mm.

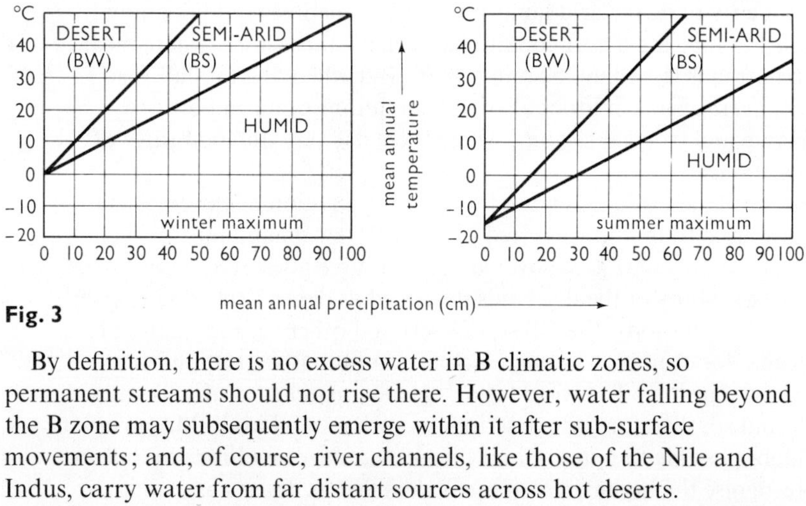

Fig. 3

By definition, there is no excess water in **B** climatic zones, so permanent streams should not rise there. However, water falling beyond the **B** zone may subsequently emerge within it after sub-surface movements; and, of course, river channels, like those of the Nile and Indus, carry water from far distant sources across hot deserts.

Despite these limitations, we will continue to describe the driest (**BW**) areas as *desert* and those corresponding to the **BS** zones as *semi-arid*.

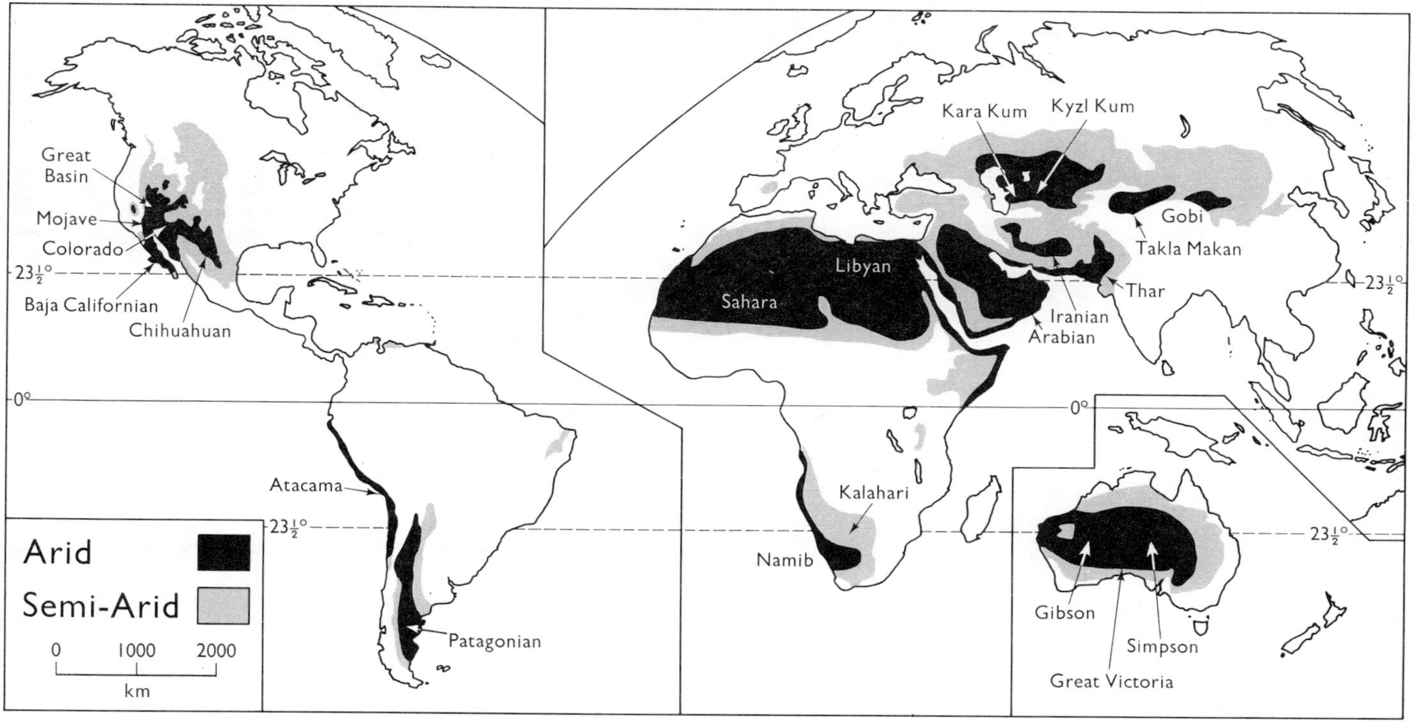

Fig. 4 These broad belts of arid and semi-arid land include many local variations in climate and vegetation. There are also numerous small dry localities with xerophytic vegetation in other places (Fig. 5); and some more extensive arid areas within mountain systems are not included—much of the Bolivian altiplano, for example.

Distribution of Arid Lands

Figs. 4 and 5 show that there are extensive arid areas in the outer tropics and sub-tropics. In these latitudes are the semi-permanent zones of high pressure, where sinking air is warmed by compression. Their influence is strongest on the western sides of the continental masses. It extends westwards over the oceans, where dry air flowing eastwards from these sub-tropical highs and the abundant insolation cause rapid surface evaporation and increase the salinity of surface waters. On the eastern sides of the continents, where the Trade Winds converge, deep moist air layers move over the surface; and, especially in eastern Asia, there are monsoonal inflows in summer.

Cold currents and upwelling cold water off the coasts of the Atacama, Namib and Lower Californian Deserts make for cooler coastal conditions and tend to accentuate the aridity. Fog formed in air chilled by the cold waters affects the coastal fringes; but as the air moves inland and is warmed, its relative humidity falls and fog vanishes.

Arid lands also occur to the lee of mountains which stand in the path of prevailing winds. As moist air moves up the windward slopes it cools slowly as condensation releases heat; but as it sinks leeward it gains heat at the more rapid, dry adiabatic rate. Even the Caribbean islands of Jamaica and Puerto Rico, where moist north-east Trades meet the eastern mountains, have rainshadow areas in the south-west, with semi-arid conditions. On a larger scale, the aridity of the USA's intermontane Great Basin and Mojave Desert is partly due to obstructing mountains, and the exceptional dryness of temperate Patagonia is caused by the Andes interrupting the flow of the westerlies.

Large areas in the interior of the continents are so far from the oceans that marine influences are very slight: another reason why in North America the sub-tropical deserts extend into higher latitudes. The dry lands of central Asia are shielded from the monsoon system of the south-east by the Himalayan barrier and the high plateaux to the north of it. Even in summer, when surface temperatures are at their highest, and a shallow low pressure system forms over central Asia, rainfall amounts are slight and evapo-transpiration losses great. In winter, the region is affected by the cold air of Asia's polar continental airmass.

Fig. 5 indicates, broadly, where aridity is promoted by the sub-tropical highs, off-shore cold currents, rainshadow effects, and continentality. But, of course, the climatic conditions are usually due to a combination of causes. There are many other small enclaves of aridity in various parts of the world.

The large desert areas associated with the sub-tropical anti-cyclones tend to give way, gradually, to less arid conditions. Polewards, they mostly shade into semi-arid winter rainfall regions. Equatorwards,

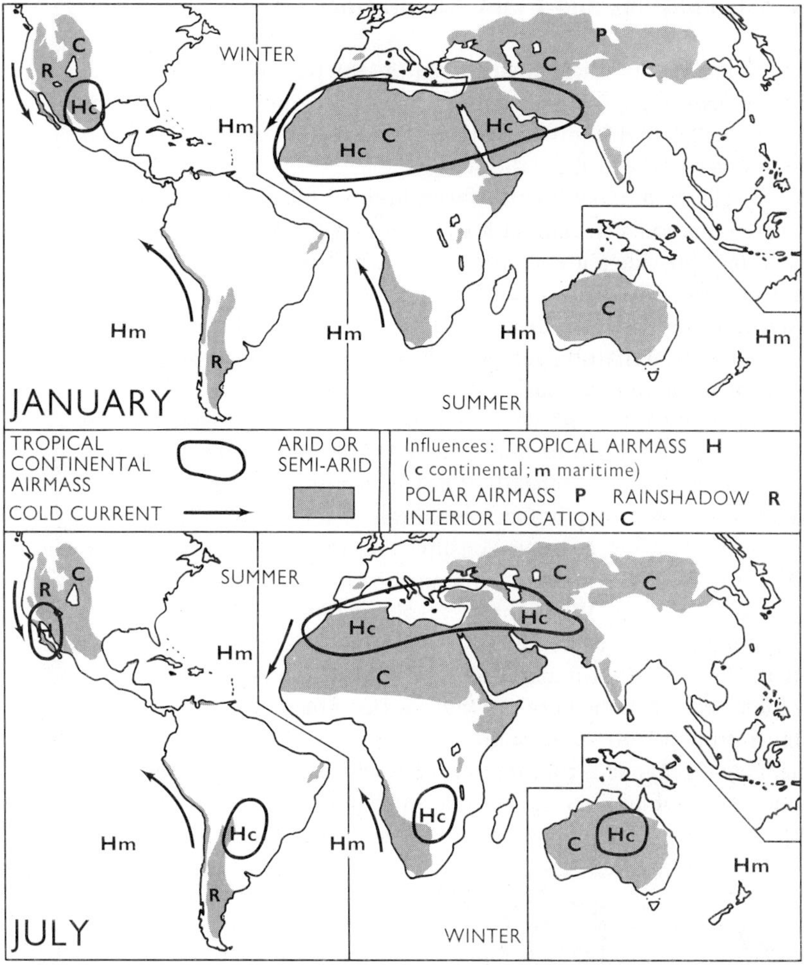

Fig. 5 The land area directly influenced by the continental airmasses is seen to vary seasonally. The maps broadly indicate where the aridity owes much to continentality (C), rainshadow effects (R), cold off-shore waters, and, in Asia, by thermal high pressure during winter (P).

where there are short periods of heavy rain in summer and long winter droughts, the soil characteristics are more typical of the dry savannas, and in Africa support large numbers of semi-nomadic pastoralists or shifting cultivators, compared with the few who occupy the truly arid lands unaffected by large-scale irrigation. But the biomass of these dry grass/semi-shrub grazing lands is very small—only some 2000 kg/ha compared with some 35 000 in moist savanna and over 250 000 kg/ha in tropical rainforests.

Desert Conditions and Plant Adaptations

Despite the harsh physical environment, many physiologically specialised plant species survive in micro-habitats. They are often hardy members of families which occur in milder neighbouring regions, adapted in form and structure to the arid conditions.

Bare rocks, boulder-strewn surfaces, hollows filled with coarse, weathered materials, accumulations of finer, wind-borne particles, and sandy dunes provide a great variety of potential sites for plants and animals to take advantage of small shaded places, cracks in rocks, or moister hollows. The soils are usually unstable, skeletal, sometimes saline and seldom mature, yet have physical and chemical properties capable of sustaining vegetation.

Despite an overall water deficiency, plants may find sufficient moisture to sustain a life cycle: from sources beneath dried-up water courses, debris-filled hollows, or beneath dunes, which often retain considerable amounts of water at depth. Occasional rain readily soaks through porous sands, whose coarseness ensures that there is little capillary rise; so that, if wind does not remove the upper sand, the lower parts remain moist for a long time. When the atmospheric humidity is high, the air surrounding grains well below the surface may also have a high water content. Thus vegetation may become established on dunes.

Some plants are ephemeral, in that they complete their life cycle during a rainy period and remain dormant in the soil as fruit or seed. Some have mechanisms that scatter seeds which embed themselves locally and so remain in a favourable environment. Other seeds are dispersed by wind; some intertwine as round wind-borne masses; those

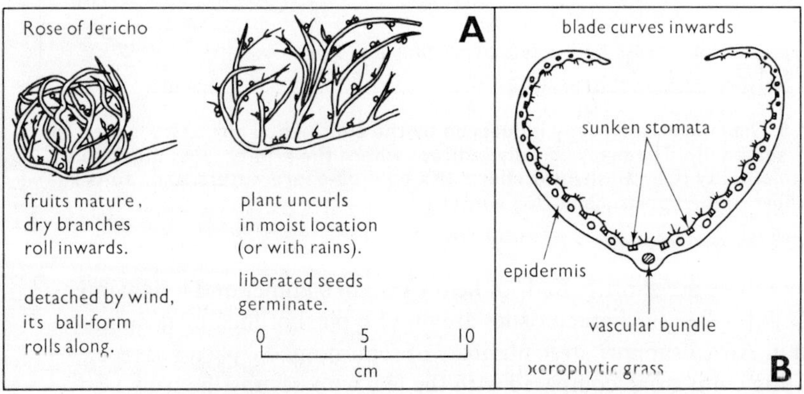

Fig. 6 (A) Rose of Jericho (*Anastatica sp.*): during drought its bracts close over and protect the small seeded fruits, even when the plant is torn away by the wind. Moisture causes them to unfurl and shed the fruits. (B) The stomata of xerophytic grasses are protected by the incurving blades.

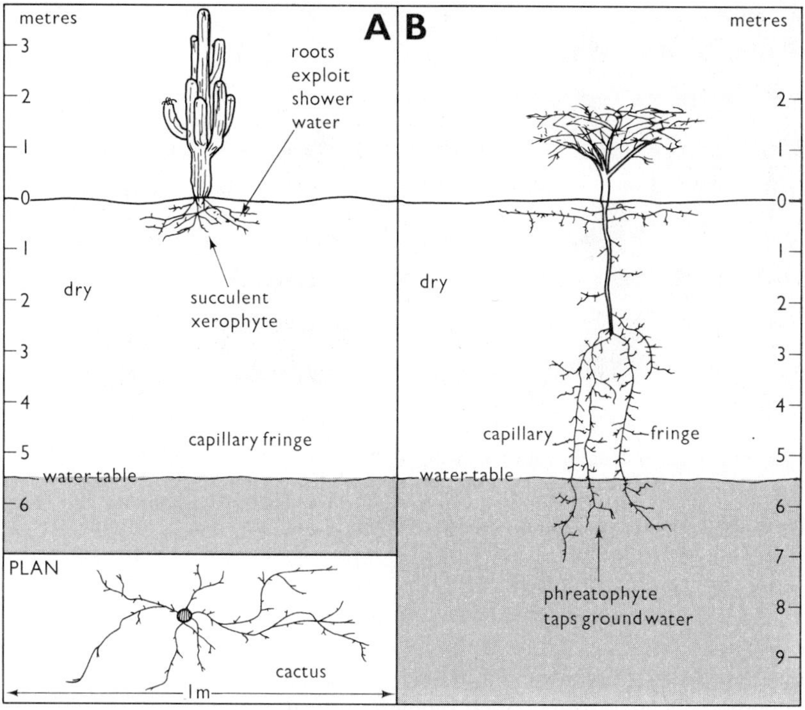

Fig. 7 (A) A succulent relying on a shallow, spreading root system to absorb storm water, and adapted to store it in its tissues. (B) A plant, such as an acacia, with a deep tap root, branching where it finds water in the capillary fringe, and with a root-spread close to the surface to obtain water after showers.

which collect in favourable hollows may germinate under moister conditions. Some lie protected by a chemical coating, until it is destroyed by moisture. In semi-arid areas, seeds with barbs or bristles may be carried and dispersed by goats and other animals.

Drought-resistant plants are called *xerophytes*, and exhibit a variety of adaptations to arid conditions. Some have long tap roots capable of reaching deep water sources; the roots of the American mesquite may extend downwards for 30 m or more. Some have branching root systems, so as to draw water from the greatest possible volume of soil. Others branch laterally over a wide area within 3–4 cm of the surface and so exploit every shower to the maximum.

Having acquired water, plants reduce its loss by a number of means. Many have very small leaves and may shed them in unfavourable periods. Their stomata, often sunken, restrict or close their openings during the heat of the day to reduce transpiration. But as this also restricts the influx of carbon dioxide, whose fixation by photosynthesis

Fig. 8 A rainshadow area in south-western Puerto Rico with xerophytic grasses, globular *Notocactus* (left), and prickly pear (*Opuntia sp.*). In these cacti, the thorns and bristles are modified shoots from their curiously shaped green stems, which are capable of photosynthesis.

provides energy and promotes growth, some plants keep their stomata open at night and take in most carbon dioxide at that time. Many xerophytes counter strong insolation by having pale leaves with reflective surfaces, and some have stomata mainly on the underside of the leaves. Small hairs and thick-walled outer (epidermal) leaf cells with waxy deposits also help to reduce water loss. The leaves of some desert grasses fold over with stomata on the inside; other grasses have leaves rolled into tubes.

The plants known as *succulents* store water in their tissues. Some, like the agave, have succulent leaves, others, such as cacti and many species of *Euphorbia*, have succulent stems, and a number have succulent roots. Most have a spreading network of shallow roots which wither during drought. Those which build up organic compounds by a night influx of carbon dioxide benefit from water produced within them when respiration breaks down the compounds. In cacti the branches are reduced to small protruberances, and leaves to spines. A small surface-to-volume ratio is helpful and is reflected by the rounded shape of many succulents, such as the barrel cacti whose stems allow photosynthesis.

While most desert plants have at least short periods of transpiration, for this is a cooling mechanism, many tolerate high tissue temperatures, and have cells adapted to combat stress caused by partial dehydration. Thicker cell walls also help to prevent rupturing. Changes in cell-sap concentration occur, which affect chemicals governing plant growth and also leaf characteristics, such as size. When drought causes a high sap concentration, any new leaves tend to be smaller and more xeromorphic. During rainy periods, when cell-sap concentration decreases, newly formed leaves are larger and allow greater transpiration, and new shoot growth is possible.

The North American creosote bush shows how shrubs can withstand heat and dessication. It has a wide-spreading, shallow root system, loses all its leaves and some branches during lengthy drought, and tolerates severe dehydration of its tissues; but some of its leaf buds remain dormant, so that new growth begins as soon as moisture is available.

An excess of salts in the soil inhibits growth in most plants, but some are salt tolerant (*halophytes*) and are able to take up salt into the cells of succulent organs until there is equilibrium with the soil solution. Soils with a very high salt content remain bare.

Semi-Arid Vegetation

In lower latitudes bordering the deserts, the sparse cover of grasses, woody plants and succulents varies in composition with soil aridity and salinity. The latter respond to minor topographical features as well as to the rainfall and its distribution. The space between plants usually reflects competition, for the bare ground is often underlain by dense, shallow root systems.

The actual composition of the vegetation usually reflects interference by men and animals, and is modified by grazing and occasional fires: such effects are described in some detail in *Tropical Savannas*[2]. Similar effects are seen along the poleward margins of the sub-tropical deserts and are considered further in *Mediterranean Environments*[3]; in each case they may lead to desertification (p. 29).

Fig. 9 Dew formed on millet leaves in the Sudan emphasises the large volume of water which may condense at night at, or near, ground level, where in arid regions it may maintain plant life and stimulate chemical weathering.

External Variables
I Climatic Influences

Radiation Gains and Losses

Over the huge desert areas which are under the influence of the sub-tropical highs, the dry sinking air diverges at low levels and prevents any extensive convergence and import of moisture. Open skies allow short-wave radiation to reach the surface readily. Long-wave energy radiated by the surface heats the air above, though some is lost direct to outer space and much is lost from the heated air itself.

Seasonal conditions vary. In summer, with a near-vertical noonday sun, the ground becomes extremely hot; bare surface temperatures may rise above 80°C, which, obviously, restricts plant and animal life. Air shade temperatures of 58°C have been recorded in Libya and Mexico. At night, while heat continues to be lost rapidly, there is no insolation and air temperatures fall sharply. Wadi Halfa in the Sudan has experienced a summer daily range of 29°C.

In winter, though the noonday sun is only some 35° above the horizon, clear skies still allow fairly high mid-day temperatures, though daylight hours are fewer. At night, ground and air temperatures may fall below freezing. Thus the daily ranges are still large; on a December day in central Libya, air temperatures have stood at −0.5°C and 37.5°C.

In the higher latitude deserts the winter temperatures may be very low indeed, especially in those lands affected by the thermal high of the Asiatic interior. Tashkent has had January days with air temperatures of −30°C and 19°C; in summer 41°C has been recorded. In America's intermontane basins air temperatures fall to −15°C and below. Frosts affect the vegetation, of course, and also increase the rate of mechanical weathering of the rocks.

The influences of the high temperatures and scarce, erratic precipitation on plant life have already been discussed. Other characteristics of the precipitation have great influence on the plant–soil system, desert morphology, and forms of land-use in arid regions.

The Nature of the Precipitation

In summer the sub-tropical highs shift polewards through several degrees, so that their lower latitude margins are affected by moister air. This is especially so on the southern fringe of the Sahara, where there is a convectional inflow towards the hot heart of the desert. The result is a

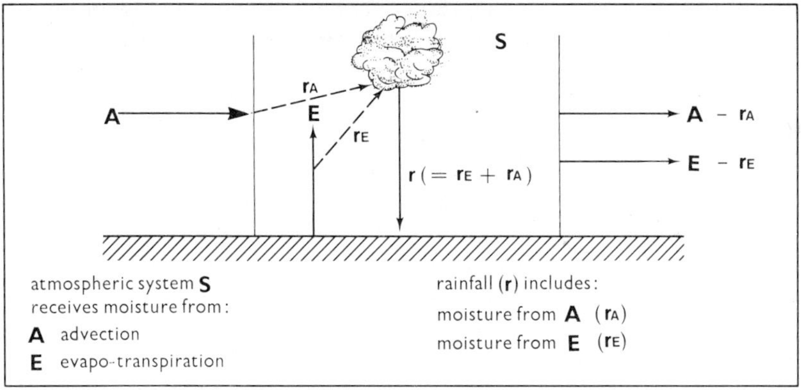

Fig. 10 External and internal exchanges of moisture in the atmosphere over a selected arid surface, where meteorological conditions allow advection.

short period of summer rain, with heavy storms, due both to strong local convection and to the wider atmospheric disturbances. Within the desert, a shallow layer of air, with properties different from those of the overlying, subsiding air mass, extends upward from the surface for some 1–2 km. In summer there is an influx of moisture at low levels; though, with such high temperatures, the *relative humidity* remains low. Strong convection movements occur over the hot surface yet, with high temperatures and the blanketing effect of the sinking upper air, clouds seldom form and rain is most infrequent. Even when towering clouds develop and rain begins to fall from a great height, it may evaporate as it descends and fail to reach the ground.

Nevertheless, unusual meteorological conditions occasionally cause torrential storms, and most parts of the deserts experience them from time to time, though many years may pass before rain falls there again. Variability in time and space is a characteristic of precipitation in the arid lands.

Some desert margins are affected by disturbances which develop in adjoining climatic zones. Cyclonic systems in the Mediterranean sometimes affect the northern Sahara and Libyan Desert and bring short periods of heavy rain and devastating floods. Tropical cyclones of great ferocity are associated with the summer monsoonal system which brings summer rains to northern and north-eastern Australia. With such heavy, erratic storms, average rainfall figures mean little. This is true of most arid regions. Virtually no rain falls in the southern parts of the Atacama Desert; and even in coastal Peru, where moisture condenses to form high stratus beneath the anticyclonic subsidence, there is usually only winter drizzle. Yet, very occasionally, as a warm sea current flows southwards along the coast, inside the cold Peru current, warm moist air brings a series of destructive storms to the coastal desert.

In most deserts, surface temperatures may fall low enough at night for heavy dew to form in the chilled surface air. This not only provides a moist micro-climate for plant life, but, like the mists and fogs of the cooler, coastal deserts, produces alternate wetting and drying, so that crystal hydration and dehydration causes rock fragmentation. Some plants thrive best where dew forms, like the *Welwitchsia mirabilis* of the Namib: condensation on its large, split curling leaves provides water for its shallow roots. The mean temperatures of arid coasts affected by cold off-shore waters, like the Atacama and Namib, are well below those of the hot desert interiors: compare summer means at Walvis Bay (Namibia), 16°C in January, with those at In Salah (Algeria), 36°C in July.

Air Movements

The wind has a drying effect and also transports and lifts the fine dry particles, separating them from the coarser surface debris. Winds are usually strongest by day, when convection is at maximum, whereas nights are relatively calm. Strong winds can produce sandstorms which advance as a wall of swirling dust. Particles may be deposited against barriers and in the lee of obstacles. Dunes of various kinds may build up in such places (p. 44) and be moved by the wind. Persistent outward movements of air transport the finest particles to semi-arid lands bordering the desert, where loess may accumulate. Great thicknesses of loess have been built up in north-eastern China. This has occurred

Fig. 11 The loess of Shensi, borne by the wind from arid lands, provided fertility for the local crops long before the tomb of the T'ang Empress Wu (d. AD 705) dominated this carefully terraced landscape. Notice the sunken courtyards of houses built into the edge of the wide transverse gulley.

intermittently, as humid and semi-arid conditions have alternated; in some periods the particles were derived from drying glacial debris. The soft, much eroded, aeolian deposits which now cover these semi-arid lands are still hundreds of metres thick.

The dry, dusty winter wind, the *harmattan*, blowing south from the Sahara, lowers the humidity in the northern and central parts of West Africa, limiting cultivation and causing unpleasant physiological effects, such as chest ailments. Strong winds may set in at times in response to distant large-scale disturbances. Dust-laden desert air is drawn into the fore of depressions moving eastward through the Mediterranean; winds known locally as the *khamsin* and *sirocco*. Within the deserts more local 'dust devils', narrow cyclonic updraughts, swirl over the heated surfaces and carry fine particles to a great height. The desert coasts are affected by land/sea breezes; very strong sea breezes daily carry fine particles far into the Namib.

As wind removes fine materials, it can create hollows through deflation (p. 43). Wind-borne particles can polish hard rock surfaces, and fret or groove rock strata by differential erosion. Mutual abrasion creates typical facets on the particles themselves. Yet the overall effect of wind as an agent of erosion in arid lands is not as great as one might imagine; many other forces create desert landforms (p. 39).

Climate and Soils

The stony surfaces and angular screes of the deserts may not form soils in the usual sense, yet contain isolated plant communities in micro-enviroments with roots extending deep into crevices. Finer, deeper mineral accumulations often have a baked surface, so that even after heavy rain infiltration is not easy. However, many plants have shallow spreading roots, and others penetrate surface cracks.

Desert soils (Aridisols) tend to be shallow and either calcareous or saline, for there are only sporadic periods of leaching and little humus. Even where water is able to infiltrate and pass through the upper soil, carbonate ions from the sub-soil, or from the rain itself, tend to build up a thick carbonate layer (caliche) where percolation ceases. Water draining into desert basins carries salt solutions from the surrounding rocks; on evaporation these remain as saline deposits. Receding, evaporating flood water may also leave salt crystals in potentially fertile soils of river flats, and salinity from rising groundwater is a threat to cultivation. Yet heat, and almost continuous sunshine, favour plant growth in these and other desert soils, provided that irrigation water is available and fresh water flooding can remove excessive salt.

Some soils, particularly in semi-arid areas, appear to be relics of those formed during previous wetter periods, when they developed a clayey

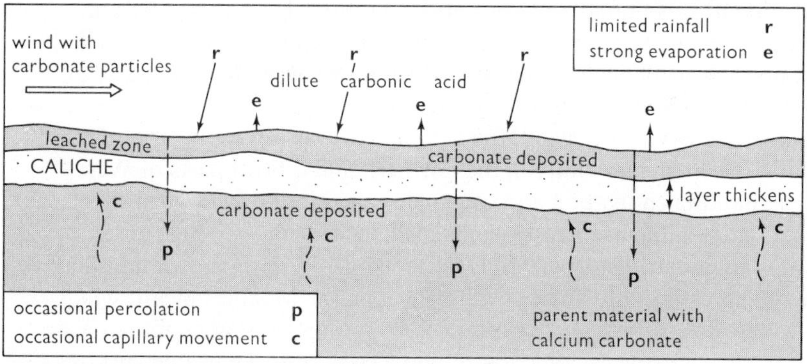

Fig. 12 Processes favouring the deposition and thickening of caliche. The mobile soil-water obtains carbonate radicals from the parent material, from atmospheric carbon dioxide and, possibly, from wind-borne deposits.

illuviated B horizon; though they, too, usually have calcareous accumulations beneath. Many of the red soils of arid Australia and the African Sahel are remnants of those developed under wetter tropical conditions: some have hardpans of lateritic origin, which may be exposed by erosion to leave a hard stony surface.

The shallow soils of the moister desert margins, which bear grasses and low shrubs, often support nomadic grazing. Where the rainfall increases, the soils, developed beneath closer grasslands with shrubs and bushes, have more humus. In Africa this has encouraged precarious settlement and farming, with closer grazing. This is also the case in central Asia, where semi-arid lands grade westwards into dry steppe, whose light brown soils have invited cereal farming. Unfortunately, large areas of these ploughed lands have been seriously eroded during periods of drought; descriptions of these dry steppes and their development are given in *Temperate Grasslands*[4]. Eastwards, in Asia, the potential fertility of the loess lands has encouraged even closer settlement, and there has been a long struggle to combat erosion by terracing and irrigation.

Past Climates

During the Pleistocene, when icesheets advanced and retreated in the higher latitudes, there were pluvial periods (with increased rainfall) in the latitudes of present hot deserts[5]. These were followed by very dry interpluvials. In one of these, about 15 000 years ago, the Sahara Desert extended far south into West Africa, where only a few forest patches existed. Before the present dry period began, about four thousand years ago, moister conditions had prevailed for some three thousand years, so that forest extended northwards and the present desert was no more than semi-arid. At this time pastoralists drew pictures of their herds on cave walls in the rugged Tibesti and Tassili hills.[6] Evidence from other

Fig. 13 An erosion gulley on the southern edge of the Sahel allows cattle to lick salt from a thick layer built up beneath the surface.

deserts shows that fluctuations of this kind have occurred throughout the world. Even during the present dry period there have been minor climatic fluctuations. The effects of the wetter periods on the desert landforms is discussed on p. 39.

Fig. 14 Sahra el-Libiya in Egypt, where sufficient water is retained beneath the sand to support vegetation. Angular blocks have fallen from the weathered, cracked rock in the foreground, exposing light interior faces which contrast with the dark desert varnish of the outer surface.

II The Influences of Local Rocks

In hot deserts the large daily variation in temperature of the rock surfaces, and the effects of crystal hydration, dehydration and oxidation make for fragmentation and disintegration. Generally, crystalline rocks, such as granites, suffer more intense weathering than compact sandstones. Their crystals, of various colours, absorb energy at different rates, causing stress through expansion and contraction. Changes of crystal size and form on hydration and dehydration also cause granular disintegration. But even chemically inert rocks may break up under large temperature changes: quartzite boulders sometimes develop cracking parallel to the surface and a maze of cracks normal to this, so that a mass of small blocks falls away. The process tends to be repeated on the exposed surface beneath. Less compact sandstones, with ample pore space, can be disrupted by crystal growth as infiltrating salt solutions evaporate.

When moisture is present, minute quantities of chemical compounds may be brought to the surface. Here iron, manganese and silicon oxides tend to be retained and build up a reddish-black coating, know as 'desert varnish'. Where moisture is sufficient, blue-green algae may colonise rock surfaces and help to mobilise and concentrate iron oxide as a rock coating.

Sedimentary rocks such as shales are affected more by frost shattering than by temperature variations above freezing. In cold winter regions, as in Mongolia and Tibet, the resulting fragmentation makes for huge scree formations at the foot of escarpments.

Various chemicals build up as crystal deposits about salt lakes and in salt pans, and have been valuable commodities over the ages. Traders carried them along caravan routes; and today railways and ships transport them from lakeside works to chemical factories. Sodium chloride, sulphate and carbonate are common deposits; some, like the valuable Dead Sea potash, are now produced by further solar evaporation; borax (sodium borate) comes from saline lakes in arid California and Nevada. The valuable nitrate deposits of arid northern Chile were formed as ammonium solutions from Andean volcanic rocks moved as groundwater into natural troughs, where they built up great thicknesses of caliche. Such mineral accumulations are the result of climatic conditions. They are both formed and preserved by the aridity; but other valuable minerals occur in desert rocks, as they do elsewhere, and may be exploited if water and energy can profitably be supplied for mining, transportation and settlement. Among the many minerals

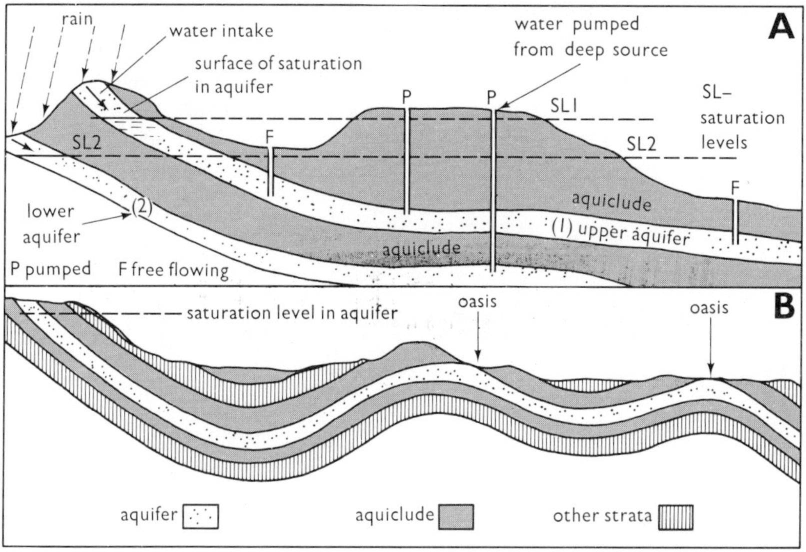

Fig. 15 Aquifers do not always conform to these simplified models. Some may exchange water with the rocks about them; others may occasionally be recharged where they are exposed at the surface, as in B.

produced from deserts are the rich iron ores from Mauritania, Western Australia and the Atacama; copper from Arizona; and the vast quantities of oil from the arid lands of the Middle East and North Africa.

The influences of particular rocks on soil formation, vegetation and cultivation are restricted by climatic conditions. So far we have seen the negative effects of chloride and carbonate deposits. However, accumulations of mixed minerals of alluvial or aeolian (wind-borne) origin, in river flats and deltas, and in desert basins, may provide the nutrients, depth and texture suitable for plant-soil systems to develop; though such deposits may also become saline with time.

The use of potentially fertile soils depends on the availability of water, so that rocks which act as groundwater storages (aquifers) are particularly important. Limestones, with their pore spaces, cracks and joints, can hold large amounts of water; and many sandstones hold water in pore spaces. Some outcrop in regions where water may soak into them, and when sandwiched between impervious rocks, which act as aquicludes, form artesian storages. These underlie many of the world's driest regions, including the Mesozoic rocks of Australia's Great Artesian Basin, the Palaeozoic limestones of Morocco's Anti-Atlas, and the Nubian sandstones of the Arabian peninsula. Here and there, the tilts and folds of basin structures bring artesian water close to the surface. Sometimes naturally eroded depressions breach the aquifers and release water; sometimes cuestas are formed from which springs emerge. Such sources form natural oases in great deserts, and, if rain recharges the aquifer, provide a sustained yield. Natural features may sometimes provide storages. In North Africa limestones, whose sub-surface caverns were formed when wetter Pleistocene conditions created karst features, are still useful water sources.

III The Biosphere—a Variety of Influences

In really arid places the vegetation is made up of relatively simple plant communities, without complex stratification. It can modify the atmosphere and soil only to a limited local extent. A mosaic of different plant communities adapted to different habitats makes up a discontinuous plant cover. As the soils are skeletal and unstable, it is difficult for the vegetation to reach a climax form without disruption.

The fauna, as well as the flora, tend to be associated with particular small environments to which they are adapted. Like the plants, and to a large extent dependent on the plants, their populations respond to the short rainy spells. Reproductive periods may be triggered by the rains and by the behaviour of plant species.

Rainfall, Plant Growth and Animal Populations

Rain can transform a desert surface in a matter of days. Ephemerals become green, develop bright flowers, and in a few weeks many will have seeded. At the same time an abundance of animal life appears. Butterflies, bees and other insects visit the flowers; caterpillars and crickets consume the ephemeral vegetation; swarms of flies appear and add to the rich food supplies for the birds, which often arrive in large numbers. Surface predators, like the spiders, scorpions and ant-lion larvae, feed on the abundance of small creatures, busy with their own responses, like the ants harvesting grass seeds.

The desert locust of northern and eastern Africa feeds on ephemeral grasses and lays its eggs in moist sand, where, after 10–20 days, green hoppers hatch out. Should the hopper population crowd the environment, they change to a darker colour and move outwards, often in millions, feeding where they can. During rainy periods, the aromatic chemicals of certain shrubs stimulate a change to a winged phase; the locusts take off

Fig. 16 The kangaroo rat feeds at night on dry vegetation and seeds. During the day it retreats to a deep, cooler burrow, for it does not sweat; but under heat stress it produces saliva which soaks the fur at its chin and throat and slightly lowers its temperature.

in swarms, which may fly downwind for thousands of kilometres. Some places, like the inner Niger floodplains in Mali, are permanent breeding grounds, and there the hopper can be controlled; elsewhere, outbreaks occur sporadically over widespread desert areas.

In semi-arid country, larger animals, like the gazelles, also respond to a limited season of plant growth, which provides food during the breeding season. Some desert rodents build up a food store in their burrows before mating, so that in dry years breeding is restricted.

Animal Adaptations to Hot, Dry Conditions

Most of the smaller creatures are nocturnal, and retreat to cracks or burrows during the day. Insects and arachnids are mainly active at night, although scorpions and others can withstand very high temperatures, and the winged creatures which cling to plants and other shaded places become active when disturbed. Burrowing animals may find a comfortable environment a metre or so down in loose material, for although surface temperatures are so high, air is a poor conductor.

Large mammals have a relatively small surface-to-volume ratio and cool as their sweat evaporates: nevertheless they, too, seek shade at the hottest time of day. Hairs trap insulating air and protect the skin from direct heat. Even so, the mammals rely on particular adaptations to reduce water loss. The camel, which drinks large amounts at irregular intervals, can endure water loss equal to a quarter of its body weight. It has a wider body temperature range than other mammals and so need not lose so much water to cool itself, though it maintains its blood volume. Its urine losses are small, and urea is used internally to make

Fig. 17 The poisonous, carnivorous Black Scorpion of the desert. Nocturnal in habit, it shelters by day in cracks and under rocks, and in extreme heat uses its large claws to burrow into sandy material.

protein. Its nasal membranes allow moist air to enter, but minimise moisture loss.

Smaller mammals, like the desert fox and Saharan hare, have large ears which give a greater cooling surface. Kangaroo rats and other small mammals, as well as desert reptiles, cool the air they exhale, and obtain water when hot, moist air, drawn into a cool nasal passage, allows condensation. Many insects and arachnids rely on an almost impervious outer skeleton to cut down water loss by transpiration. But here there is space only to touch on the numerous, varied individual adaptations, more fully described in biologies of arid zones.

Particular desert habitats support particular communities. In the cactus/creosote-bush/bur sage country of arid Arizona, holes in the giant cactus are occupied by woodpeckers, various owls, and flycatchers. A species of wren lives in a smaller cactus. The bushes are not important food sources for birds and 70 per cent of them are carnivorous or insectivorous, living on snakes, lizards, small mammals and insects.[7]

Man in the Arid Lands: Various Levels of Activity

The effects of people on the arid and semi-arid lands may be seen at three overlapping cultural/technological levels.

(1) Small groups of people, like the bushmen of the Kalahari and the Australian aborigines, skilled in locating and obtaining scarce groundwater and moist plant organs, have lived a semi-nomadic food-gathering and hunting life, and have adapted to their environment with

remarkable efficiency; dwindling numbers continue the traditional activities.

(2) By contrast, there are still large numbers of pastoral nomads in the dry lands of northern Arabia, the Sahel, northern Kenya and elsewhere: many are semi-nomads who, in the course of their annual wanderings, seasonally cultivate selected areas, such as river flats. Like the commercial nomads engaged in buying, carrying and selling, and the shifting cultivators of the more humid margins, they respond to physical conditions by mobility.

(3) Many millions live a settled life in a relatively moist environment within an arid zone—about an oasis, on a floodplain or delta, or in an area irrigated by water brought from afar. Here levels of technology overlap. For millenia, people have used simple technology, in such forms as the shadouf and Persian wheel, to supply water through channel systems to their fields, relying on the energy of men and animals. Today, others use modern machinery and mechanically generated energy to irrigate large areas, often hundreds of kilometres from a water source.

Over the years, the hunter-gatherers have had little lasting impact on their broad environment; whereas pastoral nomads and shifting cultivators have greatly affected the natural flora and fauna. Their over-grazing and over-cultivation are still actively extending the desert at the expense of dry savanna and steppe. Irrigation, with its associated land-use and settlement, has changed entire ecosystems, and ecological repercussions have been felt far from the irrigated areas (p. 34).

Pastoral Nomadism

Many nomads still live in a truly arid environment, but have modified their traditional ways. The Tuareg once ranged widely over the central Sahara, but today live mostly in the Aïr, Tibesti and Hoggar plateaux and in northern Nigeria. Family groups move with camels, cattle, goats and sheep along dried watercourses and through depressions where thin, wiry grasses, thornbush, and scattered shrubs support their livestock for a short period. Every few weeks the group moves to new pastures and waterholes. Because of the unreliable rainfall, the routes change from year to year and they continuously probe ahead to confirm their next movements. Each of the various animals can survive by grazing different types of plant from the others, enabling the group to make the most of the scarce vegetation. Once the Tuareg traded salt and dates in marginal market towns and returned with millet, leather, cloth, brassware and weapons. They dominated Saharan commerce until the advent of trading companies with modern transport. They owned land in oases, though their slaves farmed it. Today, many are turning to farm small rented plots and palm groves, or associate themselves with tourism.[8]

Fig. 18 Nomadic Tuareg who moved into the drought-stricken Sahel in Niger received relief food; but their goats soon stripped the remains of tree savanna from a sandy, stony surface already devoid of grass.

In the semi-arid lands, large numbers of nomadic pastoralists still depend on their successful adaptation to the seasonal changes in vegetation, especially in the great dry zone south of the Sahara, which runs westwards from the Sudan, across the Sahel to the Atlantic. Unfortunately, drought can still be disastrous, and between 1968–73 continuous drought afflicted this semi-arid zone. Paradoxically, the magnitude of the disaster was increased by improved means of obtaining water. During the preceding forty years, a period of reasonably reliable rainfall, many new wells were dug. The population increased by a third, and the cattle, regarded as units of wealth, doubled in number. Though water supplies improved, the capacity of the grazing lands did not. There was already erosion about the water sites, and the drought brought tremendous losses to the over-stocked lands. Many people starved and large numbers moved southwards.

In fact, the recently independent states encourage settlement, for nomads, independent in outlook and accustomed to crossing state boundaries, can be a nuisance. But those who abandon nomadic life to settle in the adjoining dry savannas add to the increasing numbers who restrict the normal practice of shifting agriculture. Sedentary farming in the dry marginal lands can so easily damage the structure of the dry soils and deplete nutrient reserves. On the dry margins of the Kalahari nomadic pastoralists disturb the fragile ecosystem by burning and over-grazing. Their boreholes lower the water-table, so that bushmen concentrate on permanent supplies, unable to hunt.

Other peoples in the dry lands of Africa and the Middle East practise semi-nomadism with transhumance, moving stock along regular routes according to seasonal conditions. In Morocco, sheep and goats are moved in early summer from the hot, dry, interior plains to the cooler, high Atlas, and return when winter rain revives the lowland vegetation. In West Africa, the nomadic Fulani move cattle, sheep and goats southwards during winter drought to graze on savannas which are, by then, relatively free of tsetse fly. They move northwards again with the summer rains. In Senegal and other parts of the Sahel the annual migration includes a period spent where the people can grow millet on river terraces during the summer rains, while their stock feeds on new natural growth.

Such traditional ways make the most dry lands, which are unable to support large populations without enormous investment. Modern technology and engineering might make the limited water reserves available, but may rapidly deplete them.

Desertification

The extension of the world's deserts by man's direct and indirect actions is known as 'desertification'—an ugly word for an ugly process. In many parts of the world deserts are being extended along the dry margins of

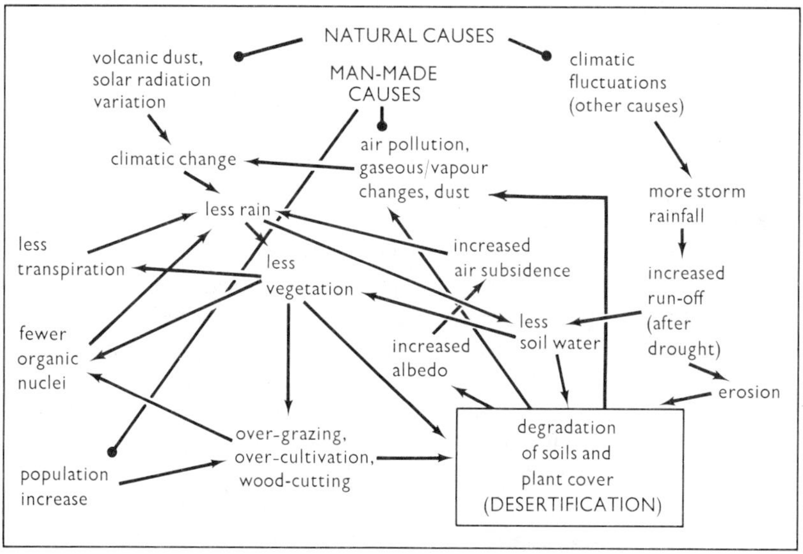

Fig. 19 A model showing chains of events stemming from natural and man-made causes which may lead to desertification. The climatic changes considered on the right are those which cause sudden torrential storms; a long-term amelioration of climate, with a higher, more reliable rainfall would, of course, have quite different consequences.

the semi-arid zones, where over-stocking destroys natural pastures. The result is an increase in the proportion of goats, whose browsing habits destroy trees, shrubs, and grass alike. Not only the desert margin suffers. Much soil deterioration and erosion occurs within the semi-arid lands themselves. This often takes place about a favourable nucleus: trampling and over-grazing about a reliable well can increase storm run-off, channel erosion and badland formation; over-cropping about a village on fertile, but dry, soil produces a zone of soil deterioration; trees and shrubs destroyed for firewood and charcoal-making despoils vegetation over a wide radius about a settlement.[9] In each case, as the cover by vegetation or crops decreases, unpalatable plant species may colonise the land, and topsoil is likely to be lost; gulleying may take place, and sometimes the wind exposes rubbly surfaces or forms dunes.

As pastoralists cause desertification they are restricted spatially, which makes for further deterioration. Yet changing to a settled life may increase the tendencies to desertification in adjoining land. The nomads of arid Rajasthan, in north-west India, have largely lost their trading and transport functions; their grazing land is restricted, and the soil deteriorates as their livestock uses the meagre water and grazing resources. Some 15 000 ha of potential grazing is being lost to desert each year. Many turn to farming in adjoining territory. But in Rajasthan, with improved medical facilities and a high birth-rate, the population is still rapidly increasing; so that whereas in 1951 the average of 14 ha of land was available per family, by 1971 this had dropped to 10 ha, and may well be 6 ha by the turn of the century[10]. More and more marginal land is being used by inexperienced farmers, so that its yield rapidly declines. More people means a greater demand for wood; more trees and shrubs are destroyed; dung is used for fuel rather than manure; so soils deteriorate and further desertification follows.

There is a conflict of ideas as to how the plight of the semi-arid lands should be tackled. Governments, receiving aid, tend to create large irrigation schemes where labour is available and transport and marketing easy to arrange. The more remote dry lands, sparsely populated by migratory people, and marginal lands with fragile soils and unreliable climate are less attractive for development. This may be a reasonable response; grandiose plans for the arid lands, such as tree-belts encircling the Sahara, or flooding large depressions to change the climate, are distrusted by many environmentalists.[5] They would prefer multiple land-use planning for the dry zones; a continuation of nomadism, with scientific control of the land; reclamation of areas affected by erosion; wildlife preservation; and controlled tourism and mineral working. The alternative is continuing desertification, with pressure coming from the increasing over-population of limited farmland in more humid, fertile regions, such as the highlands of Kenya.

Fig. 20 In Egypt thousands of years of flooding and water control, as here at Sakkara, have allowed cultivation to support civilisation in an almost rainless desert. Modern technology allows greater control of the Nile waters, for irrigation and energy, but has had less desirable side-effects (p. 36).

Thus investment in the latter might well ease the pressure on dry marginal lands.

Not all arid and semi-arid land lies in developing countries. But richer nations can draw on state capital or private investment to provide water, irrigate suitable land, supply energy and materials for settlement schemes, and exploit potential mineral wealth. This, of course, also applies to the oil-rich states of the arid Middle East. In each case, of course, water supply is the prime essential.

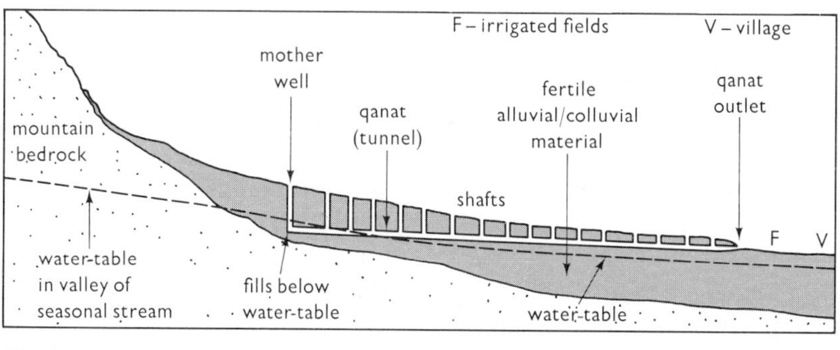

Fig. 21 A qanat system designed to carry water from mountain sources to areas with fertile land but a low natural water-table.

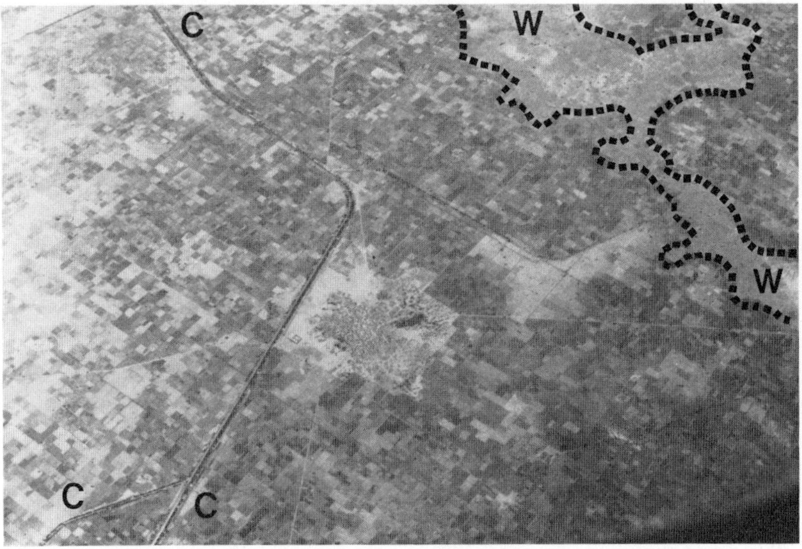

Fig. 22 Canals C–C, over 50 m wide, carry water from the Indus system across the northern plains. Tube wells provide additional water for these closely settled farmlands. Old water courses, like W–W, are flooded during the wet monsoon. They are grazed rather than cultivated and have little settlement.

Irrigation over the Centuries

For many millenia the people who settled at oases, about springs, or along river floodplains have used simple technology to raise and distribute water locally, and have created elaborate constructions, such as aqueducts, for wider distribution. Underground channels, *qanats*, developed long ago in Central Asia and Iran, are still widely used in the Middle East to tap groundwater at the foot of mountains and carry it great distances through gently sloping tunnels to emerge on the edge of fertile, but arid land. Fig. 21 shows the shafts made during construction, which are now used to keep the channel clear. Evaporation losses are minimal, though some water is lost by infiltration.

Other irrigation methods have continued down the centuries: the use of shallow, gravity-fed channels, blocked by mud packing as required; and where floods bring water and fine alluvium to the fields, earth is banked up about small plots to retain water as long as possible. To conserve supplies, people have used cisterns, underground caverns, depressions dug to catch run-off and retain water moving by gravity through the sub-soil, and have created lakes during the rains by blocking stream beds with boulders and earth dams. Such methods are in general use today: but the scale and materials used have changed with energy generation and new technology. Electric or diesel pumps raise groundwater from greater depths; massive dams create deep lakes

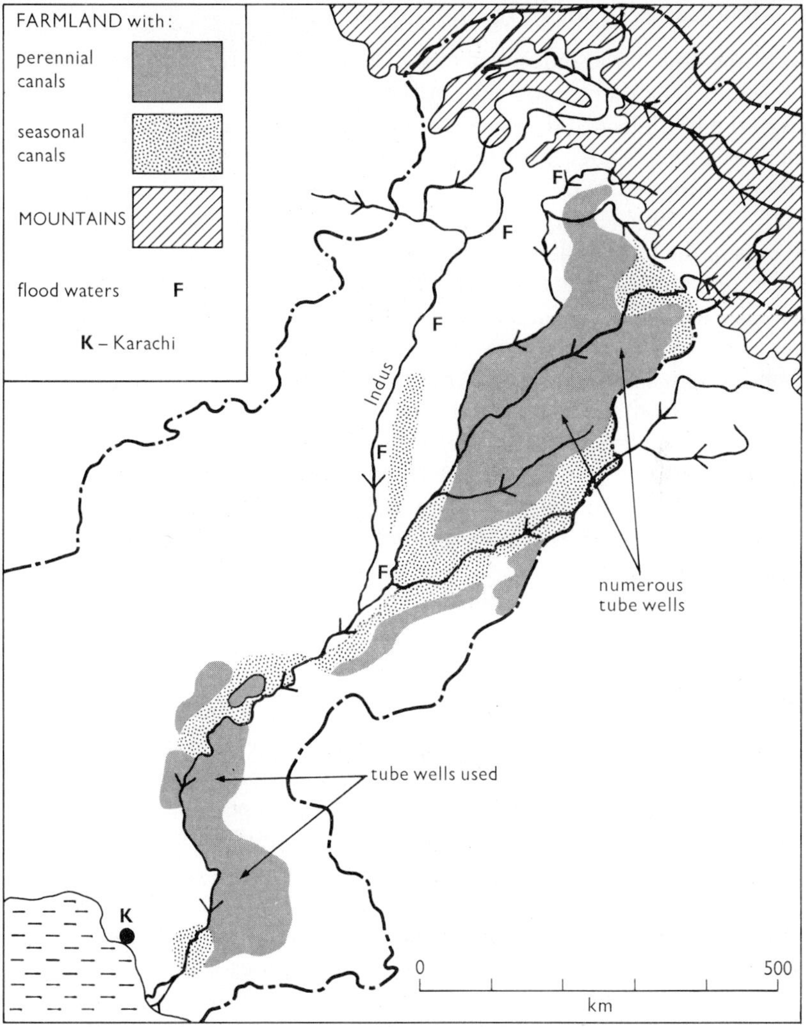

Fig. 23 In Pakistan, the progressive development of the Indus and its tributaries, and especially the provision of perennial canals and tube wells, allows tens of millions of people to farm in an otherwise arid environment.

stretching back hundreds of kilometres; machines excavate and line canals and create networks of irrigation channels. Metal pipelines of decreasing diameter carry water from reservoir to the field, and release it through nozzles, or tiny drip feeds, to the plants. Fig. 23 shows the general methods of irrigation used in Pakistan, whose chief climatic characteristic is aridity. There the whole hydrological system of a huge river, the Indus, has been transformed, as engineering systems have evolved progressively to control and distribute the waters. [11]

The Advantages of an Irrigation System

Most of the flow in the Indus system is from catchment in the Himalayas and foothills. The monsoon breaks in June and rivers reach peak flood-levels in the foothills in July–August: a flood wave passes downriver, to reach Sind a month later. From September the river levels fall, until snow-melt brings a rise in March.

Early in the 19th century, inundation canals were built to carry water from cuts in the bank to land parallel with the river. During the mid-19th century, gated barrages were contructed across rivers to raise the water level and allow accumulations of alluvium to pass downstream. Water could now be diverted throughout the year, greatly extending the area under both summer and winter crops. Large canals were built to transfer water from the western rivers to supplement those further east. More recently, high dams in the mountains have provided storage and hydro-electricity. Most of the cropped land is now served by perennial canals; while, at the same time, shallow wells draw fresh water from river floodplains and from the extensive groundwater reservoir beneath the north-eastern plainlands. Thus, despite the aridity, over half Pakistan's workforce is engaged in agriculture.

Some Disadvantages

The water that allows tens of millions to live in villages and towns amid agricultural land has also created problems of waterlogging and saline accumulation. Water not used by crops or lost by evapo-transpiration, or drained away, accumulates as rising groundwater, until it reaches root level or even forms a surface swamp. In desert conditions soils rapidly acquire salt from the evaporation of dilute saline irrigation water. In some areas sub-surface water moving down-gradient from distant irrigated areas, accumulates where it meets natural rock or man-made impediment and so rises. Such surplus water has usually acquired more salt as it slowly moves through the ground, and eventually becomes too saline for crops to tolerate. Today tube wells are commonly used to pump saline groundwater to rivers and canals, which dilute it; thus the water-table is lowered from the crops under irrigation. But, of course, this uses expensive energy.

In Israel, where wells have tended to become saline, water is fed into boreholes during the annual winter abundance, creating a fresher underground storage and raising the water-table. In other parts of the world where large artesian reserves are tapped, the water, long underground, is often saline, and may only suit crops such as alfalfa, widely grown for fodder, which can tolerate a fairly high salt content. Elsewhere, artesian water has proved suitable for a variety of crops; but

Fig. 24 Arable land in the lower Indus valley which has become encrusted with salt and now bears halophytic shrubs. Excessive irrigation upstream has caused groundwater, which has become saline, to rise to the surface and evaporate.

Fig. 25 Australian aborigines picking canteloupe melons on the southern edge of the Gibson Desert, where groundwater is pumped up and distributed through channels lined with plastic sheeting. The air temperature is 50°C, so that direct loss by evaporation is very great, and undesirable in an area where the water-table has been falling.

it is a resource whose reserves are not always known, and which is only slowly replaced. Even small irrigation schemes in Western Australia have lowered the water-table sufficiently to affect the pumped supplies on which the stock depends; and short-term farming projects in Baja California accept that the wells will dry up after ten years or so. But circumstances vary: intensive date farming in parts of Tunisia is threatened by an annual 5 cm fall in the water-table, yet the huge alfalfa-sheep schemes in southern Libya pump water from 200 m down at a rate which should enable reserves to last several hundred years.[12]

Other water control and irrigation schemes have their drawbacks. Dams and diversions along the Egyptian Nile have created enough irrigated land to make the country self-sufficient in wheat and an exporter of rice, and to produce abundant hydro-electricity; but there have been ecological repercussions. Floodplains downriver, deprived of alluvium and its nutrients, now need much fertiliser. In the delta, the shoreline has retreated, and groundwater levels have fallen, so that salt water has penetrated the coastland.

Irrigation increases the dangers from infections, notably from bilharzia. This is carried by freshwater snails, which release larvae able to infect the people using the water. In West Africa, exposed water surfaces encourage blackflies which transmit river blindness[13]; and though there are dust and flies throughout the arid lands, flies are often pestilential at oases. Where all-the-year-round cultivation replaces cropping with a dry fallow period, crop pests may thrive on perennial food sources. There are also many instances of plant pests and diseases being carried along water channels.

Wealth from the Arid Lands—Large-scale Investments

So far we have considered irrigation projects in developing countries. Different patterns of settlement are seen in those arid lands, such as Arizona and California, where large amounts of investment capital and energy go into intensive, irrigated, specialised crop production. In California this is in the hands of a few firms controlling farmers' output and organising canning, processing and despatch. Highly mechanised agriculture, and transport systems with negotiated freight rates, are part of what is often called 'factory farming'. Water and energy are received in quantity from distant sources. California's irrigated deserts and southern cities are supplied through canals and pipes from the Colorado river system, and from wetter temperate lands to the north-west, as well as from more local sources.

In developing and developed countries alike, mineral resources in arid locations will be worked if there is the demand. Investments in water supplies, mines, mining settlements, transport and communications lead

Fig. 26 In the hot, dry Kalgoorlie region of Western Australia huge investment has developed nickel mines and air-conditioned townships; as here at Kambalda on the edge of Lake Lefroy, a salt pan occupying an 80 km long depression.

to the establishment of townships in absolute desert which may thrive as long as resources and demands last. Such are the Middle Eastern oil cities, Chilean copper towns, and the air-conditioned townships of Western Australian iron and nickel mines.

There are usually difficulties in meeting demands for fresh fruit and vegetables. But mineral wealth may be re-invested in *hydroponic cultivation*. This involves irrigating the roots of plants growing in sand by raising a water-table containing selected nutrients in solution. High yields can be obtained and, as the surface remains dry, little water is lost by evaporation.

Desalination and other Water Sources; Water Conservation

Salt water reserves are abundant in the seas bordering deserts and as saline water underlying arid lands. Desalination plants can each produce millions of gallons of fresh water a day. Most use distillation, transforming water to steam, which condenses to fresh water in cooling stages and leaves concentrated brine to be removed. Some rely entirely on oil- or gas-burners to produce heat, others incorporate compressors, and a few use pumps to lower pressure. A different method allows ice to form, leaving brine behind. Electrodialysis is also used, causing sodium and chlorine ions to pass through separate membranes, away from the fresh water. Reverse osmosis under pressure is also used to force the water in brine through a membrane which holds back the salt.

Kuwait, Abu Dhabi and other Middle Eastern capitals use gas for sea-water distillation[14]. All these processes consume a great deal of energy. Methods of efficiently concentrating solar energy, in these lands with little cloud, have practical problems, though there are already small, successfully combined solar power and desalination plants.

Glacial masses are seriously considered as possible sources of fresh water for the world's deserts. Scientists are investigating the feasibility of capturing icebergs formed in Antarctica, towing them northwards and anchoring them off the desert coasts of Australia, the Americas and Arabia; melt-water would then be pumped ashore. Alternatives involve pumping fresh water from beneath Antarctic ice-shelves to fill rubber pod tanks at a floating base, and then towing them to where required. Certainly ice is a huge potential resource, and necessary capital inputs may well compare favourably with those required to create large water supplies from other sources.

We not only need to provide more water, but to make more efficient use of what there is. New methods of water conservation may have as great an effect as major supply projects. They include carefully calculated drip irrigation, the use of mulches, or sheeting, to reduce evaporation from soil surfaces, mono-molecular films to cover large water surfaces, chemical anti-transpirants to induce plant stomata closure, and the development of crop strains to withstand aridity and salinity.

Fig. 27 The Sahra el–' Arabiya in Egypt; here deep dry wadis wind below the dissected edge of gently tilted plateaux, whose surfaces also bear incised water channels. Today, occasional storms fill the wadis with fierce, but short-lived torrents; but the overall pattern of drainage was developed in a previous humid period.

IV The Effects of Morphogenic Processes

The present evolution of arid landforms is often affected by events which occurred long ago, even on the geological time-scale. Geological processes in the distant past have created recognisable features in the present arid lands which influence current processes. Immense areas of ancient rocks, planed down to form shields of moderate relief, make up a large part of the Sahara, Arabian peninsula, Thar Desert, and central and western Australia. By contrast, there are dry mountainous lands: in North America, for example, where uplift and fracturing have created basins which are bordered by characteristic piedmonts and contain depositional landforms related to drainage from the mountains.

Past climatological conditions are reflected in desert landforms, many of which began to develop during pluvial periods several thousand years ago. Channels which were once part of a perennial drainage system now receive the run-off from torrential storms, unhindered by vegetation. Vertical erosion deepens gorge-like wadis, which wind along the original courses, and lateral abrasion keeps the sides steep. Flash floods fill the wadis in a few hours and subside as quickly, leaving deep alluvial debris over the wadi floor; though wind deflation may later remove much fine surface material. Such streams that emerge from wadis percolate into the desert and dry up by rapid evaporation.

Surface channels on the old shields often lead into inland drainage depressions, such as that containing Lake Chad. Some 50 000 years ago Lake Chad occupied a vast area, when its surface stood over 100 m above its present level. It shrank during the dry conditions which

Fig. 28 In this northern part of the Atacama, the mountains of the Peruvian coastal region bear no vegetation under present climatic conditions, yet dramatically demonstrate the effects of erosion by running water.

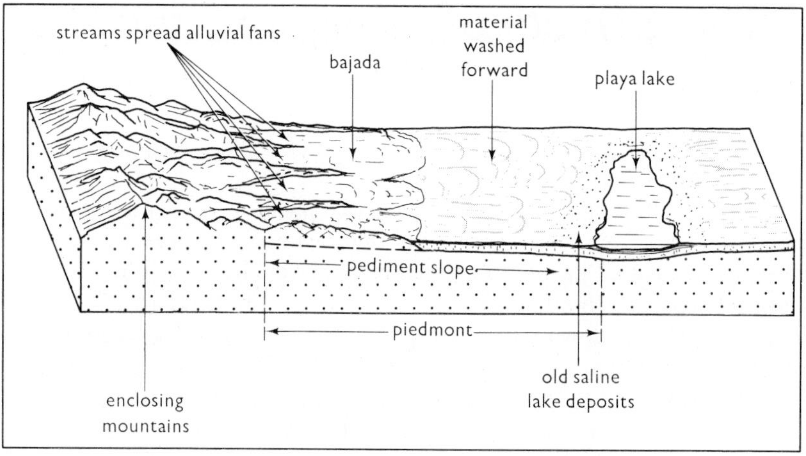

Fig. 29 A section of one side of a basin with inland drainage. Under arid conditions there is only occasional stream flow from the mountain valleys.

followed, and large dunes built up over parts of its bed. As the waters rose again these were covered, though some form islands in the present, smaller lake.

Lakes in enclosed basins in the type of mountain country so common in south-western USA have also varied in size with climatic conditions, which have affected the amounts of material washed into the basins. Today, high strand lines and salt flats about the lakes indicate previous water levels. Many of these lake depressions have been filled by materials washed forward from the foot of the enclosing mountains, where

Fig. 30 The small mesa, with coarse scree below its crumbling face, is a relic of the surface seen in the foreground, where herbs are rooted among the weathered rock. Dark shrubs grow on the gentle debris-covered slopes which extend from the base of these features.

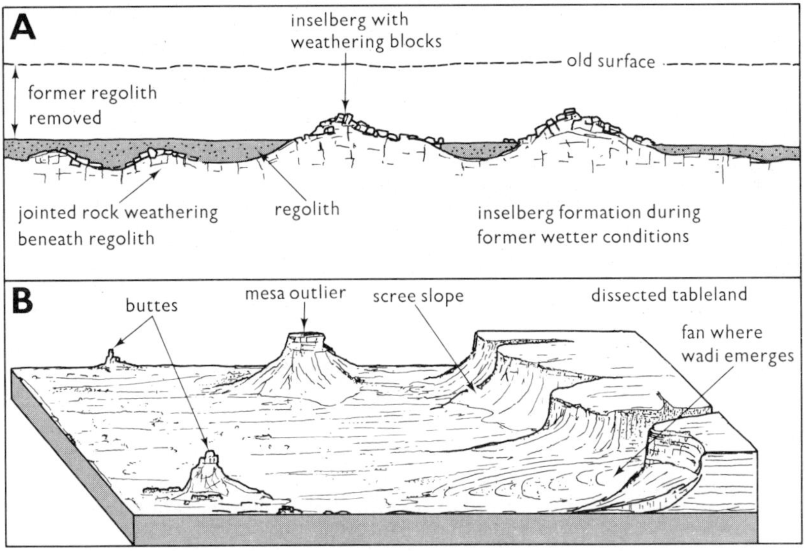

Fig. 31 (A) The piles of jointed rocks which, weathered deep beneath a moist regolith, were exhumed by erosion under humid conditions. Climatic change may make them part of an arid landscape. (B) A surface with outliers left by a retreat of a tableland, which is itself dissected by an old drainage system.

streams entering the basin have deposited their load and created fans. In some the fans have coalesced to form masses of material known as a *bajada*. Some of this washes forward over the pediment which slopes gently inwards from the piedmont. Water also continues to move as sporadic surface or sub-surface flow towards the centre of the basin.

Fig. 32 Rounded inselbergs rise from the Tanzanian tableland, whose aridity is indicated by tall succulent euphorbia. Weathering detaches curving slabs from rock masses which were rounded and jointed before emergence.

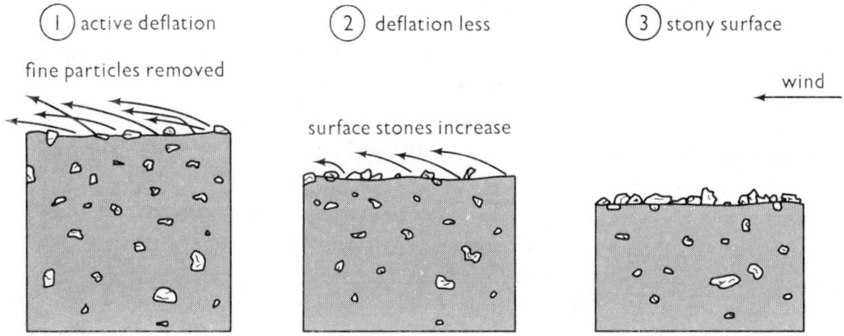

Fig. 33 The wind removes the fine materials, and deflation continues until an accumulation of stones virtually blankets the surface.

Cone-shaped alluvial fans are common desert forms, especially where drainage channels emerge from uplands on to flat lowlands. There are, in fact, many broken uplands, even in broad deserts with low relief overall. In Libya and Egypt, for example, there are sandstone plateaux, showing various levels of planation, and dissected by deep wadi systems. Their stream-dissected scarps overlook the older plains, where detached outliers form mesas, buttes and pinnacles. Isolated masses are features of

Fig. 34 (*Left*) In arid Western Australia wind action causing deflation, and wash during occasional storms, have left a stony surface; strips of bare ground lie in the lee of mallee bushes. (*Right*) Part of a dry pediplain in north-west Australia where stones ranging from 2–8 cm across cover the surface of the sandy debris in which they were embedded.

Fig. 35 An accumulation of crescent dunes at Liwa in Abu Dhabi, with gentle, roughly parallel, windward slopes and steep lee faces.

all these arid plains of ancient rocks. Some narrow inselbergs are survivors of dissected surfaces whose edges have receded by parallel retreat, leaving gently sloping erosional plains. Some are the remains of jointed rocks which, under humid conditions, weathered into boulders beneath a moist regolith, which has since been removed. These processes are described in more detail in *Tropical Savannas*[2].

Some desert masses are structured forms related to very old planed-down rocks, as in the Hoggar mountains in the Sahara, where ancient granites and gneisses form a massif some 2000 m high, though much of the surface is now covered by thick lavas, weathered into blocks and pinnacles.

By no means all the gentler desert surfaces are sandy. Much of the North African desert is covered with an angular stony mantle (*reg*), resembling the stony gibber tracts of central Australia. These are mainly due to wind deflation which has winnowed out the finer particles. Storm flood waters may also periodically sweep smaller material into adjoining depressions. Alternate wetting and drying, and in cold deserts freezing and thawing, cause volume changes, so that stones move upward through a thick mantle of debris to the surface. In semi-arid regions, deflation may remove dry particles covering a moister sub-surface horizon and eventually form a wide 'deflation hollow', perhaps a metre deep.

Sand in the arid lands may be derived from the erosion of sandstones, from the granular disintegration of granites and other crystalline rocks, from old alluvial deposits, or, locally, from coastal sources. Wind-borne grains work on structural weaknesses and, being effective at low levels, sometimes leave surface ridges elongated in the direction of the wind; they also undercut cliffs and rock pillars.

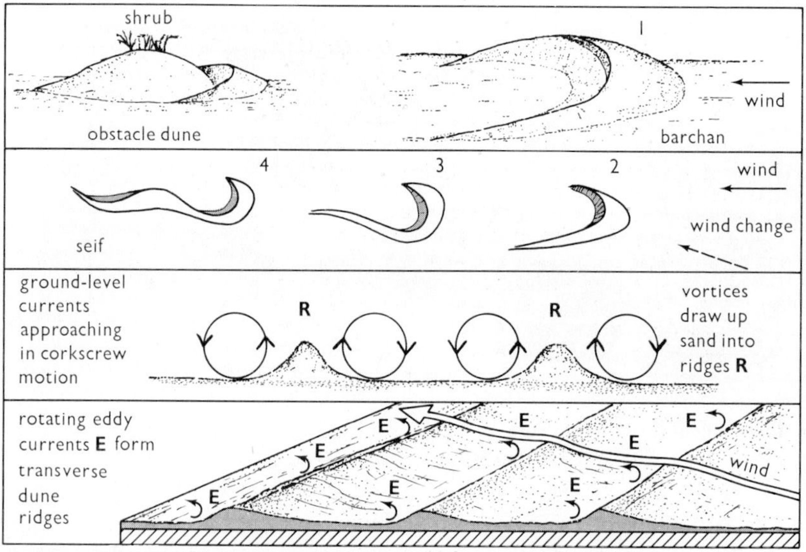

Fig. 36 Types of dune formation. The barchan, affected by a cross-wind, is seen to develop by stages (2–4) into a seif dune. Other elongated ridges are formed by the longitudinal vortex flow developed in wind streams. Transverse dunes tend to occur on great sand accumulations; eddying helps to maintain a contrast between the gentle windward slopes and steep lee faces.

The great sand accumulations (*ergs*) have a variety of forms. Air flowing over sand generally carries the finest particles in suspension; moves the medium-size ones by a series of leaps (saltation), involving lift, forward movement, and return to the surface; and rolls along the coarser ones. Small turbulences in air flow cause ripples on the surface.

The lower wind speed in the lee of an obstruction is the cause of deposition and dune formation. At a certain dune height, grains are removed from the windward face and sand-slips occur down the lee slope, causing the dune slowly to advance. Even on a hard rock surface, a sand patch may initiate deposition and dune building. Wind carries the sides of the dune forward as the arms of the typical crescent *barchan*, whose lee face is usually steepened by wind eddying.

A persistent change in wind direction may extend one arm of a barchan into a long ridge which, linking with others, creates longitudinal *seif* dunes. The dune patterns are often complex. In some sandy deserts, longitudinal dunes, parallel to the wind direction, meet other lines of dunes and create pyramidal, star-like masses. Oblique dunes may be due to wind-flow patterns or to underlying topography, or to their interactions. In many deserts, particularly in central Australia, vegetation has stabilised dunes over a wide area. Dune stabilisation may be induced on a local scale by such techniques as bitumen spraying, which reduces mobility and provides plant nourishment.

References

[1]D. C. MONEY (1978) Climate, Soils and Vegetation (UTP)
[2]D. C. MONEY (1980) Tropical Savannas (Evans)
[3]D. C. MONEY (1982) Mediterranean Environments (Evans)
[4]D. C. MONEY (1980) Temperate Grasslands (Evans)
[5]K. HARE (1977) Man Gets His Deserts (desertification) *Geog. Mag.* **49** p. 705
[6]A. T. GROVE (1977) Climate for Deserts *Geog. Mag.* **49** p. 634
[7]V. E. SHELFORD (1978) The Ecology of North America (Univ. of Illinois) p. 373 *et seq*
[8]J. KEENAN (1974) An Era Ends for Tuareg Nomads *Geog. Mag.* **44** p. 465
[9]A. WARREN (1977) Landscapes in Despair (desertification) *Geog. Mag.* **49** p. 631
[10]S. P. MALHOTRA (1977) An Overcrowded Desert (Rajasthan) *Geog. Mag.* **50** p. 102
[11]B. L. C. JOHNSON (1979) Pakistan (Heinemann) p. 64 *et seq*
[12]K. ATKINSON *et al* (1972) Man-made Oases of Libya *Geog. Mag.* **45** p. 112
[13]J. WILLIAMS (1974) Scourge of Sahel Rivers *Geog. Mag.* **47** p. 78
[14]H. BOWEN-JONES (1980) Ancient Oman is Transformed *Geog. Mag.* **52** p. 286

Other Sources

J. L. CLOUDSLEY-THOMPSON (1977) Man and the Biology of Arid Zones (Arnold)
R. U. COOKE & A. WARREN (1973) Geomorphology in Deserts (Batsford)
H. DREGNE (1977) Degradation by Degrees (amount of desertification) *Geog. Mag.* **49** p. 708
A. GOUDIE & J. WILKINSON (1977) The Warm Desert Environment (CUP)
R. HANBURY-TENISON (1980) Stay at Home Life for Kalahari Bushmen *Geog. Mag.* **53** p. 111
D. NIR (1974) The Semi-Arid World (Longman)
J. SCHECHTER (1977) The Negev Life-style *Geog. Mag.* **50** p. 101
J. TIVY (1979) Biogeography (Oliver and Boyd)
H. WALTER (1979) Vegetation of the Earth (Springer-Verlag, New York)

Points for Discussion

1 Reasons for difficulties in defining 'arid lands'.

2 Relationships between the source regions of air masses and the present distribution of the world's arid lands.

3 The extent and distribution of the world's deserts change from time to time. The importance of considering such changes within different time scales.

4 Desert life forms exhibit a great variety of adaptations to their environment.

5 Even a short rainy spell may stimulate great activity in desert life forms and may rapidly transform the appearance of a bare surface.

6 Though no rain falls, air humidity may still affect desert vegetation and geomorphological processes.

7 The present arid landforms owe much to geomorphological processes in the past.

8 Semi-nomadic pastoralism represents a sensible adaptation to conditions in the desert margin/dry savanna lands.

9 Man's efforts to improve the forms of land-use in arid and semi-arid lands often have unforeseen ecological repercussions.

10 In semi-arid lands an apparent advantage such as a water source, locally fertile soils, or a nodal routeway location may prove to be a mixed blessing.

11 Problems resulting from long-continued, large-scale irrigation.

12 The feasibility of using the world's water resources to make productive a large proportion of the arid wastelands.

13 A number of important mineral resources are peculiar to desert lands or to rocks formed under desert conditions.

14 The wind is responsible for many different types of desert surface.

15 Differences between dry lands in temperate interior locations and those in the sub-tropics.

16 The study of relatively small systems is particularly appropriate and advantageous in the arid lands.

Glossary

adiabatic process causing changes in a rising or falling mass of air without transfer of energy from its surroundings
aeolian related to the wind
air mass a large air body of considerable depth in which horizontal temperature and humidity gradients are relatively slight
albedo a measure of the ability of a surface to reflect insolation
anticyclone (high) a mass of subsiding air creating high pressure; the outward flowing air moves clockwise about it in the northern hemisphere
aquiclude a rock impervious to water from the surface or from adjoining water-bearing rocks
aquifer a rock which holds and permits the passage of water
arachnid a small animal with body in two parts and four pairs of legs
Aridisol a soil of arid environment; many are immature or skeletal, with low organic content and salts accumulated in their profile
artesian water water in an aquifer which will rise to the surface in a well
bajada (bahada) alluvial fans joined to form a continuous apron of waste along the foot of a mountain
barchan a crescent-shaped dune with points advanced by wind in the direction of dune movement
biomass the total plant and animal material in a given system (stated as dry weight)
calcareous containing calcium carbonate
caliche a near-surface layer cemented by precipitated calcium or magnesium carbonates (in Chile: alluvium cemented with sodium nitrate and chloride)
capillary rise solution drawn up a narrow pore or soil space by the attraction of the denser solid that surrounds it
climax vegetation the final composition of plant communities developed from colonisation to a state of approximate equilibrium with the environment
crystal hydration molecules of water combine with the crystal of a salt and change its form and volume
cuesta a ridge of steep descent on one side and gentle descent on the other
deflation the removal of relatively fine particles by the wind, lowering the surface or creating a hollow
ecosystem a complex integrated system in which living communities and their non-living environment interact
ephemeral a plant with a brief life cycle
evapo-transpiration the combined loss of water from surfaces and by transpiration from plants
granular disintegration the breakdown of a rock leaves its component crystals as grains
halophyte a salt-tolerant plant
humus a substance produced by the slow decomposition and oxidation of organic matter on, or near, the surface
hydrological concerned with water, from its precipitation to its eventual return to the atmosphere by evaporation—thus including run-off and groundwater movements
illuviated material moved, usually in solution, from an upper to lower horizon in the soil profile
ion an atom, or group of atoms, positively charged through losing electrons (cation) or negatively charged through gaining electrons (anion)
inselberg an isolated rock mass, massive or of huge boulders
insolation energy radiated by the sun
interpluvial a dry period between wetter ones
karst limestone affected by severe weathering; fluted, fretted and containing shafts, caverns and pits
lateritic hardpan a surface, or near-surface crust, hardened by iron-rich solutions brought up during drought and evaporated and oxidised on drying
leaching removal of soil materials in solutions by percolating water
lithological concerned with rock structure and composition
loess an accumulation of minute material, usually of silt-size particles, carried by the wind and deposited

monomolecular film a chemical film which spreads over water covering it to the thickness of a single molecule, minimising water loss by evaporation
nitrifying conversion of nitrogen or nitrogen compounds to substances which can be used in biological processes
organic acid one derived from the decomposition of living matter (as opposed to the wider chemical definition)
osmosis the movement of solvent molecules (usually water) from a dilute to a more concentrated solution through a selectively permeable membrane
pediment gently sloping, debris-strewn, eroded rock platform adjoining a scarp face or mountain slope
photosynthesis the conversion of carbon dioxide and water into organic compounds by solar energy and plant chlorophyll
phreatophyte plant with long tap root which extends into, or near, the water-table
piedmont 'at the foot of the mountain': sometimes applied to low-angled pediment surface stretching away from slope; also to general slopes away from mountain
playa shallow salty lake in enclosed area of inland drainage
Pleistocene geological period, of 1–2 million years, which included the glacials and interglacials of the most recent Ice Age
pluvial a period with plentiful rainfall
protoplasm the fluid making up the cells of living organisms; it contains proteins
regolith a mantle of debris and material weathered from and covering the bedrock
saltation the forward movement of a particle along a surface by a series of skips or jumps
soil horizon a horizontal layer of variable depth with properties differing from the soil above and beneath
stomata the pores in the epidermis of parts of plants which allow gaseous exchange to occur
succulent a plant which stores water in its tissues
transhumance a regular movement of pastoralists and stock between areas seasonally favourable for grazing
tsetse fly a scourge of bush savanna which causes wasting disease in hooved animals and sleeping sickness in man
xeromorphic an adaptation of form to allow survival during drought
xerophyte a plant able to withstand drought due to special modifications